MORAL ALPHABET

WITH ILLUSTRATIONS

BY

B. B.

Authors of "The Bad Child's Book

of Beasts"

"More Beasts for Worse Children"
"The Modern Traveller" etc.

Hilaire Belloc

[ZHINGOORA BOOKS]

This edition is published by
Zhingoora Books.

The Cover is Designed by Pallav Sethiya.

zhingoora_books@yahoo.com

A

stands for

Archibald who told no lies,
And got this lovely volume for a prize.

The Upper School had combed and oiled their hair,
And all the Parents of the Boys were there.
In words that ring like thunder through the Hall,
Draw tears from some and loud applause from all,—
The Pedagogue, with Pardonable Joy,
Bestows the Gift upon the Radiant Boy:—

"Accept the Noblest Work produced as yet"
(Says he) "upon the English Alphabet;
"Next term I shall examine you, to find
"If you have read it thoroughly. So mind!"
And while the Boys and Parents cheered so loud,
That out of doors

a large and anxious crowd
Had gathered and was blocking up the street,
The admirable child resumed his seat.

Moral.

Learn from this justly irritating Youth,
To brush your Hair and Teeth and tell the Truth.

B stands for Bear.

When Bears are seen
Approaching in the distance,
Make up your mind at once between
Retreat and Armed Resistance.

A Gentleman remained to fight—
With what result for him?
The Bear, with ill-concealed delight,
Devoured him, Limb by Limb.

Another Person turned and ran;
He ran extremely hard:
The Bear was faster than the Man,
And beat him by a yard.

Moral.

Decisive action in the hour of need
Denotes the Hero, but does not succeed.

C stands for Cobra; when the Cobra

bites
An Indian Judge, the Judge spends restless nights.

Moral.

This creature, though disgusting and appalling,
Conveys no kind of Moral worth recalling.

D

The Dreadful

Dinotherium he
Will have to do his best for D.
The early world observed with awe
His back, indented like a saw.
His look was gay, his voice was strong;
His tail was neither short nor long;
His trunk, or elongated nose,
Was not so large as some suppose;
His teeth, as all the world allows,
Were graminivorous, like a cow's.
He therefore should have wished to pass
Long peaceful nights upon the Grass,
But being mad the brute preferred
To roost in branches, like a bird.[A]
A creature heavier than a whale,
You see at once, could hardly fail
To suffer badly when he slid
And tumbled

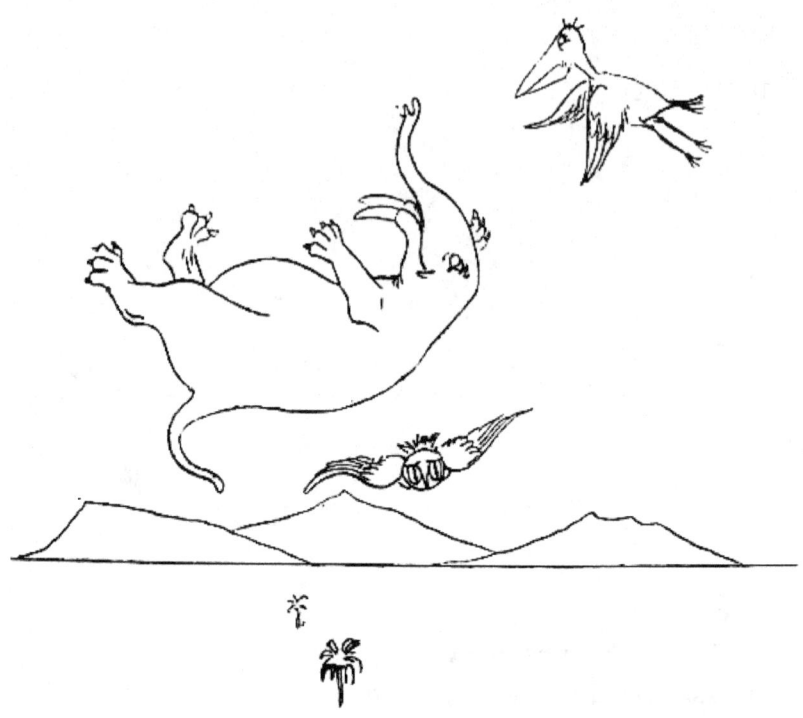

(as he always did).
His fossil, therefore, comes to light
All broken up: and serve him right.

Moral.

If you were born to walk the ground,
Remain there; do not fool around.

[A]
We have good reason to suppose
He did so, from his claw-like toes.

E

stands for

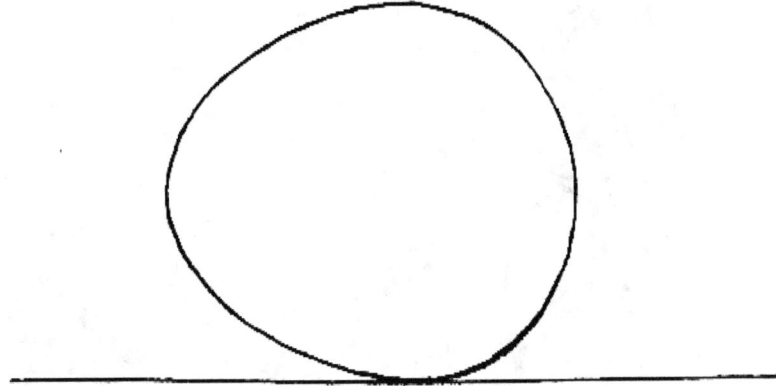

Egg.

Moral.

The Moral of this verse
Is applicable to the Young. Be terse.

F

for a

Family taking a walk
In Arcadia Terrace, no doubt:
The parents indulge in intelligent talk,
While the children they gambol about.
At a quarter-past six they return to their tea,
Of a kind that would hardly be tempting to me,
Though my appetite passes belief.
There is Jam, Ginger Beer, Buttered Toast, Marmalade,
With a Cold Leg of Mutton and Warm Lemonade,
And a large Pigeon Pie very skilfully made
To consist almost wholly of Beef.

Moral.

A Respectable Family taking the air
Is a subject on which I could dwell;
It contains all the morals that ever there were,
And it sets an example as well.

G

stands for Gnu, whose weapons of Defence
Are long, sharp, curling Horns, and Common-sense.
To these he adds a Name so short and strong,

An Uitlander.

That even Hardy Boers pronounce it wrong.
How often on a bright Autumnal day
The Pious people of Pretoria say,
"Come, let us hunt the——" Then no more is heard
But Sounds of Strong Men struggling with a word.
Meanwhile, the distant Gnu with grateful eyes
Observes his opportunity, and flies.

Moral.

Child, if you have a rummy kind of name,
Remember to be thankful for the same.

H   was a

Horseman who rode to the meet,
And talked of the Pads of the fox as his "feet"—
An error which furnished subscribers with grounds
For refusing to make him a Master of Hounds.
He gave way thereupon to so fearful a rage,
That he sold up his Stable and went on the Stage,
And had all the success that a man could desire
In creating the Part of

"The Old English Squire."

Moral.

In the Learned Professions, a person should know
The advantage of having two strings to his bow.

I
the Poor Indian, justly called "The Poor,"

He has to eat his Dinner off the floor.

Moral.

The Moral these delightful lines afford
Is: "Living cheaply is its own reward."

J

stands for James, who thought it immaterial
To pay his taxes, Local or Imperial.
In vain the Mother wept, the Wife implored,
James only yawned as though a trifle bored.

The Tax Collector called again, but he
Was met with Persiflage and Repartee.

When James was hauled before the learned Judge,
Who lectured him, he loudly whispered, "Fudge!"
The Judge was startled from his usual calm,
He

struck the desk before him with his palm,
And roared in tones to make the boldest quail,
"*J stands for James*, it also stands for jail."
And therefore, on a dark and dreadful day,
Policemen came and took him all away.

Moral.

The fate of James is typical, and shows
How little mercy people can expect
Who will not pay their taxes; (saving those
To which they conscientiously object.)

K

for the Klondyke, a Country of Gold,
Where the winters are often excessively cold;
Where the lawn every morning is covered with rime,
And skating continues for years at a time.
Do you think that a Climate can conquer the grit
Of the Sons of the West? Not a bit! Not a bit!
When the weather looks nippy, the bold Pioneers
Put on two pairs of Stockings and cover their ears,
And roam through the drear Hyperborean dales
With a vast apparatus of Buckets and Pails;

Or wander through wild Hyperborean glades
With Hoes, Hammers, Pickaxes, Matlocks and Spades.
There are some who give rise to exuberant mirth
By turning up nothing but bushels of earth,
While those who have little cause excellent fun
By attempting to pilfer from those who have none.
At times the reward they will get for their pains
Is to strike very tempting auriferous veins;

Or, a shaft being sunk for some miles in the ground,
Not infrequently nuggets of value are found.
They bring us the gold when their labours are ended,
And we—after thanking them prettily—spend it.

Moral.

Just you work for Humanity, never you mind
If Humanity seems to have left you behind.

L

was a Lady, Advancing in Age,
Who drove in her carriage and six,
With a Couple of Footmen a Coachman and Page,
Who were all of them regular bricks.

If the Coach ran away, or was smashed by a Dray,
Or got into collisions and blocks,
The Page, with a courtesy rare for his years,
Would leap to the ground with inspiriting cheers,
While the Footman allayed her legitimate fears,
And the Coachman sat tight on his box.
At night as they met round an excellent meal,
They would take it in turn to observe:
"What a Lady indeed! . . . what a presence to Feel! . . ."
"What a Woman to worship and serve! . . ."

But, perhaps, the most poignant of all their delights
Was to stand in a rapturous Dream
When she spoke to them kindly on Saturday Nights,
And said "They deserved her Esteem."

Moral.

Now observe the Reward of these dutiful lives:
At the end of their Loyal Career
They each had a Lodge at the end of the drives,
And she left them a Hundred a Year.
Remember from this to be properly vexed
When the newspaper editors say,

That "The type of society shown in the Text
"Is rapidly passing away."

M

was a Millionaire who sat at Table,
And ate like this—

as long as he was able;
At half-past twelve the waiters turned him out:
He lived impoverished and died of gout.

Moral.

Disgusting exhibition! Have a care
When, later on, you are a Millionaire,
To rise from table feeling you could still
Take something more, and not be really ill.

N

stands for Ned, Maria's younger brother,

Who, walking one way, chose to gaze the other.
In Blandford Square—a crowded part of town—
Two People on a tandem knocked him down;
Whereat

a Motor Car, with warning shout,
Ran right on top and turned him inside out:
The damages that he obtained from these
Maintained him all his life in cultured ease.

Moral.

The law protects you. Go your gentle way:
The Other Man has always got to Pay.

O

stands for Oxford. Hail! Salubrious seat
Of learning! Academical Retreat!
Home of my Middle Age! Malarial Spot
Which People call Medeeval (though it's not).
The marshes in the neighbourhood can vie
With Cambridge, but the town itself is dry,
And serves to make a kind of Fold or Pen

Wherein to herd a lot of Learned Men.
Were I to write but half of what they know,
It would exhaust the space reserved for "O";
And, as my book must not be over big,
I turn at once to "P," which stands for Pig.

Moral.

Be taught by this to speak with moderation
Of places where, with decent application,
One gets a good, sound, middle-class education.

P

stands for Pig, as I remarked before,
A second cousin to the Huge Wild Boar.
But Pigs are civilized, while Huge Wild Boars

Live savagely, at random, out of doors,
And, in their coarse contempt for dainty foods,
Subsist on Truffles, which they find in woods.
Not so the cultivated Pig, who feels
The need of several courses at his meals,
But wrongly thinks it does not matter whether
He takes them one by one

or all together.
Hence, Pigs devour, from lack of self-respect,
What Epicures would certainly reject.

Moral.

Learn from the Pig to take whatever Fate
Or Elder Persons heap upon your plate.

Q

for Quinine, which children take

With Jam and little bits of cake.

Moral.

How idiotic! Can Quinine
Replace Cold Baths and Sound Hygiene?

R

the Reviewer,

reviewing my book,
At which he had barely intended to look;
But the very first lines upon "A" were enough
To convince him the *Verses* were excellent stuff.
So he wrote, without stopping, for several days

In terms of extreme, but well-merited Praise.
To quote but one Passage: "No Person" (says he),
"Will be really content without purchasing three,
"While a Parent will send for a dozen or more,
"And strew them about on the Nursery Floor.
"The Versification might call for some strictures
"Were it not for its singular wit; while the Pictures,
"Tho' the handling of line is a little defective,
"Make up amply in *verve* what they lack in perspective."

Moral.

The habit of constantly telling the Truth
Will lend an additional lustre to Youth.

S

stands for Snail, who, though he be the least,
Is not an uninstructive Hornèd Beast.

His eyes are on his Horns, and when you shout
Or tickle them, the Horns go in and out.
Had Providence seen proper to endow
The furious Unicorn or sober Cow
With such a gift the one would never now
Appear so commonplace on Coats of Arms.
And what a fortune for our failing farms
If circus managers, with wealth untold,
Would take the Cows for half their weight in gold!

Moral.

Learn from the Snail to take reproof with patience,
And not put out your Horns on all occasions.

T

for the Genial Tourist, who resides
In Peckham, where he writes Italian Guides.

Moral.

Learn from this information not to cavil
At slight mistakes in books on foreign travel.

U

for the Upas Tree,

that casts a blight
On those that pull their sisters' hair, and fight.

But oh! the Good! They wander undismayed,
And (as the Subtle Artist has portrayed)
Dispend the golden hours at play beneath its shade.[B]

Moral.

Dear Reader, if you chance to catch a sight
Of Upas Trees, betake yourself to flight.

[B]
A friend of mine, a Botanist, believes
That Good can even browse upon its leaves.
I doubt it. . . .

V for

the unobtrusive Volunteer,
Who fills the Armies of the World with fear.

Moral.

Seek with the Volunteer to put aside
The empty Pomp of Military Pride.

W

My little victim, let me trouble you
To fix your active mind on W.

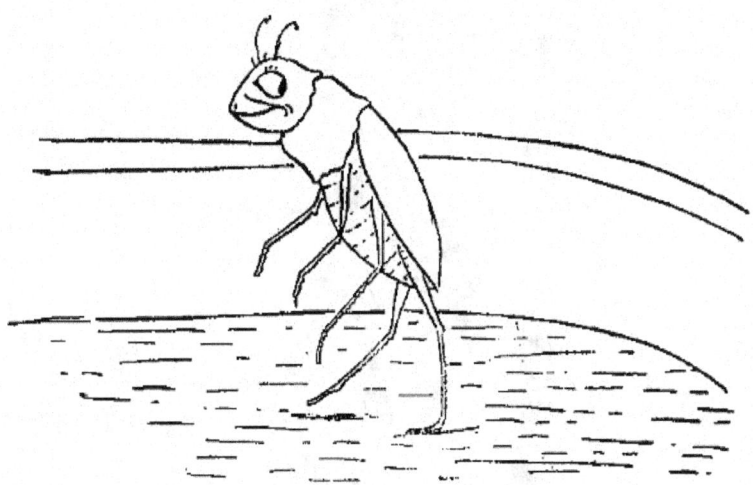

The waterbeetle here shall teach
A sermon far beyond your reach:
He flabbergasts the Human Race
By gliding on the water's face
With ease, celerity, and grace;
But if he ever stopped to think
Of how he did it, he would sink.

Moral.

Don't ask Questions!

X

No reasonable little Child expects
A Grown-up Man to make a rhyme on X.

Moral.

These verses teach a clever child to find
Excuse for doing all that he's inclined.

Y

stands for Youth (it would have stood for Yak,
But that I wrote about him two years back).
Youth is the pleasant springtime of our days,
As Dante so mellifluously says

(Who always speaks of Youth with proper praise).
You have not got to Youth, but when you do
You'll find what He and I have said is true.

Moral.

Youth's excellence should teach the Modern Wit
First to be Young, and then to boast of it.

Z

for this Zébu, who (like all Zebús)[C]
Is held divine by scrupulous Hindoos.

Moral.
Idolatry, as you are well aware,
Is highly reprehensible. But there,
We needn't bother,—when we get to Z
Our interest in the Alphabet is dead.

[C]
Von Kettner writes it "Zébu"; Wurst "Zebu":
I split the difference and use the two.

The End